D1156540

Old Faithful Inn

at Yellowstone National Park

by Christine Barnes

Photography by Fred Pflughoft & David Morris

W.W.WEST

First Edition
Published by W.W.West, Inc., 20875 Sholes Rd., Bend, Oregon

Copyright 2001 Text by Christine Barnes
Copyright 2001 Photos by photographers credited

Book Design: Linda McCray

Copy Editor: Barbara Fifer

All rights reserved. No portion of this book may be reproduced in any form, including electronic, without written permission of the publisher.

Publisher's Cataloging-in-Publication Data

Barnes, Christine 1947-
    Old Faithful Inn at Yellowstone National Park/Christine Barnes
    photographs by Fred Pflughoft and David Morris--1st edition
        p.cm.
        includes bibliographical references
        ISBN 0-9653924-4-9

1. National Parks and Reserves--West (U.S.) 2. Historical Buildings--West (U.S.)
3. Hotels--West (U.S.) Guidebooks I. Title

Library of Congress catalog card number 00-133880

Printed in Hong Kong by C & C Offset Printing Co. LTD.

The Greatest Show on Earth 9

Old Faithful Inn 27

New and Old Architecture 53

Yellowstone National Park 57

Selected Bibliography 62

Travel Information 63

P.T. Barnum dubbed his circus "The Greatest Show on Earth" when it opened in Brooklyn, New York, in 1871, but in the far reaches of the Northwest Wyoming Territory was nature's Greatest Show on Earth. Instead of elephants and tigers under a big top, bison, bear, elk, moose, coyotes and wolves roamed the mountainous, deeply gorged, geyser-studded landscape.

It was land so important, so astounding, and so unusual that on March 1, 1872, the United States Congress decided to preserve it. Yellowstone National Park was the first awe-inspiring chunk of America designated as a national park.

The "Act of Dedication," as the Congressional bill was called, set aside "...as a public park or pleasuring ground for the benefit and enjoyment of the people" and "for the preservation, from injury or spoilation, of all timber, mineral deposits, natural curiosities, or wonders...."

It was an odd event for the times, and definitely an odd place. The final spike of the first transcontinental railroad line linking the established East with the West Coast had been driven three years earlier. While tales of the volcanic craters had circulated since the 1810s, the first official exploration of the Yellowstone region was the 1869 Cook-Folsom-Peterson

Cliff Geyser in Black Sand Basin is unpredictable, but when it erupts the geyser's water rises twenty-five to thirty-three feet for several hours at a time, above. Majestic Castle Geyser in the Upper Geyser Basin, facing page, is the largest cone geyser in the park.
Fred Pflughoft

Expedition, followed the next year by the Washburn-Langford-Doane Expedition. (Nathaniel Langford later became the first superintendent of Yellowstone National Park.) Two surveys conducted by Ferdinand Hayden, head of the U.S. Geological Survey of the Territories, one in 1871 and another in 1872, were the first Congressionally funded expeditions.

While the Hayden Survey gathered hundreds of specimens and documented the natural resources and curiosities, it also concluded that the land was of little value for anything but "recreation and geologic study." Hayden found the area too rugged and erratic for grazing, and its sparse timber stands of poor quality for harvesting. As for valuable minerals like those that created the California gold rush, he found little future in mining the region.

What Hayden did find was wonder after natural wonder; the geologist was totally smitten. Well into the journey, the party reached the Upper Geyser Basin. On August 4, 1871, he wrote: "Early in the morning, as we were leaving the valley, the

Firehole River cuts through a canyon of the same name northwest of Old Faithful, left. Grand Canyon of Yellowstone National Park is one of the park's most spectacular sights and the subject of Thomas Moran's best-known painting, following pages. Fred Pflughoft

grand old geyser which stands sentinel at the head of the valley gave us a magnificent parting display, and with little or no preliminary warning it shot up a column of water 6 feet in diameter to the height of 100 to 150 feet...This is one of the most accommodating geysers in the basin, and during our stay played once an hour quite regularly. On account of its apparent regularity, and its position overlooking the valley, it was called by Messrs. Langford and Doane 'Old Faithful'."

Scribner's Monthly ran stories from both Hayden's and Langford's journals and reports. Other newspaper and magazine accounts of the wild landscape tantalized readers still in the grips of the Victorian era. Photographer William Henry Jackson documented the 1871 and 1872 Hayden Surveys, and landscape painter and illustrator Thomas Moran, subsidized by *Scribner's* and the Northern Pacific Railway, also joined the Hayden party. What words could not describe, photographs and paintings did.

Moran's major piece from the expedition, *The Grand Canyon of the Yellowstone,* was unveiled at a New York party hosted by the Northern Pacific Railway in May following the formation of Yellowstone as a national park. Instead of featuring spewing geysers and mud pots, Moran's huge canvas captured the Yellowstone River's Lower Falls and Grand Canyon. Magnificent, yes; terrifying, no. Here was a park for the people.

Management of the park was put under the Secretary of the Interior. His responsibility was twofold: to protect the miraculous, seemingly sacred land and wildlife and to make it accessible to the public. Wildlife had long made the exotic landscape home, but man used the region as well. Native peoples, including Crow, Blackfeet, Bannock, Shoshone and Nez Perce tribes, were warm-season occupants. Even after the formation of the park,

William W. Wylie began guiding tourists through Yellowstone in the 1880s. His "permanent camps" were not popular with park administrators, but they filled the growing need for tourist accommodations.
Colorado Historical Society

hunters and trappers virtually had free rein in killing the wildlife, and hunting continued until passage of the Lacey Act in 1894.

As the first national park in America—actually in the world—there was no model to follow. No rules or regulations came with the designation, but the bill did include the power to grant leases on "small parcels of land" for buildings and accommodations.

Early "pioneer tourists" usually entered the park from Montana, having been outfitted in Bozeman or Virginia City. A journey into Yellowstone was not for the faint of heart. Camping in the wilderness and running into some of the wild-looking—and sometimes acting—mountain men, a few Indians and perhaps a thief all added to the real adventure of a trip. Yet early journals portray tourists who shrugged off the discomfort and even danger for the opportunity to be part of the country's national treasure.

Managing the park was a difficult task, and by 1886 the U.S. Army was put in charge, to control the souvenir-hunters,

The Mammoth area with its fifty hot springs, primal colors and terraces draw both wildlife, like these elk, and two-legged visitors. John L. Hinderman

poachers and bandits. Almost as difficult was granting leases for construction of accommodations. Well-to-do visitors arrived by rail at the park's North Entrance beginning in 1883 and transferred to horse-drawn "tally-ho" stagecoaches to continue their journey.

Primitive tent compounds provided early park accommodations. From 1883 to 1891, the Yellowstone Park Association, a subsidiary of the Northern Pacific Railway, built hotels along Yellowstone's Grand Loop Road. The early roads were something to contend with, and by 1883 the situation was so bad that Congress passed a bill to provide road and bridge construction under the supervision of an

Early tourists traveled to the Upper Geyser Basin, *facing page*, where springs and geothermal sites mingled like these along the Firehole River. Today, park visitors can travel along Firehole Lake Drive where the Terraces of Great Fountain Geyser are found, *below*, or exchange glances with a yellow-bellied marmot, *right*. Fred Pflughoft

engineer officer assigned by the Secretary of War.

Visitors, not content with a side trip to Old Faithful Geyser, wanted a place to spend the night within the wildly exotic Upper Geyser Basin. In 1884, the first lunch station/hotel, a ramshackle building dubbed "the shack," was built. It burned in 1894, and an equally sad wood building was constructed in its place. In 1899, the acting park superintendent noted in his annual report that the "system of hotels should include one at the Upper Geyser Basin....An opportunity to see some of the greatest geysers in action is often lost to tourists by their not being able to stay over night here."

The bugle of the bull elk signals the advent of fall in Yellowstone.
John L. Hinderman

Mismanagement and financial woes plagued the companies attempting to run the facilities. The Northern Pacific, inter- ested in securing its position at the park, eventually bought majority stock in the Yellowstone Park Association (earlier YPIC).

In the spring of 1901, the railroad sold its controlling stock in the Yellowstone Park Association to Harry Child, Edward W. Bach and Silas Huntley, owners of the Yellowstone Transportation Company. The hope was that the new owners would work with the railroad to bring tourists to the park via the Northern Pacific line. Child was soon named president of the association and became a powerful force at Yellowstone and in Washington, D.C.

High on his list of priorities was to have a hotel built at the Upper Geyser Basin. Park regulations required structures to be

The sun rises over Yellowstone Lake lifting the curtain to another perfect day. Fred Pflughoft

one-quarter mile from a natural object of interest—but officials of the Yellowstone Park Association wanted the new hotel to be closer to Old Faithful Geyser. In 1894, a new regulation allowed building one-eighth mile from the geyser. Still, it was four years before an architect designed a hotel for the site. The Department of the Interior approved A.W. Spalding's plans for a Queen Anne style hotel, but nothing happened. By 1900, frustrated Department of Interior officials were pressing for construction of a hotel.

Spalding's plans were never executed next to the most famous geyser in Yellowstone National Park. Instead, Harry Child hired Robert Reamer, an Ohio native and self-taught architect, to design a grand hotel more fitting to the exotic setting.

The ornate travertine formations of Minerva Terraces are part of Mammoth Hot Springs, left. Thermal pools of West Thumb Geyser Basin reflect the afternoon clouds at Yellowstone National Park, following pages. Fred Pflughoft

Old Faithful Inn, with its steeply pitched roof and rustic architecture, set the tone for national park lodge design when it opened in June 1904. Fred Pflughoft

Architect Robert Reamer was a master of observation. Old Faithful Inn is an architectural wonder, but the real brilliance is Reamer's understanding of the power of its setting. In 1902, when this relatively unknown architect began designing the Inn, he understood the draw of nature. The landscape introduces his creation built of the rough-and-tumble materials of the region. The quirky oddities of the park itself are reflected in every nook of the Inn.

Perhaps sensitive to its unusual appearance, the Northern Pacific Railway's early "Through Wonderland" brochure explained: "The Inn is not in the least a freaky affair, pertinent to its locality. It is a thoroughly modern and artistic structure in every respect—modern in its appointments and artistic in the carrying out of an unconventional and original scheme."

Artistic, modern and unconventional, the Inn was not only rooted in the landscape, but was also designed with high drama in mind. A towering gable roof dominates the original portion of the Inn, which is called the Old House.

The steeply pitched roof reflects the shape of P.T. Barnum's big-top tent. Flagpoles line the widow's walk built along the peak, emphasizing that this is a house of entertainment. In the early days, guests climbed through the lobby stairway and the suspended balconies, through the crow's nest and onto the roof for a 360-degree view of the Upper Geyser Basin. A spotlight on the widow's walk pointed out

Horse-drawn tally-ho coaches, surreys and pack animals hauled visitors over the bumpy roads of Yellowstone until officials could no longer ignore progress. The Secretary of the Interior announced that on August 1, 1915 privately owned automobiles would be allowed in Yellowstone National Park, J.E. Haynes #31398

erupting geysers and prowling bears attracted to garbage, much like a ringmaster highlighting circus acts.

"A geyser seen in eruption under the searchlight is a most remarkable sight," a 1905 Northern Pacific Railway brochure exclaimed. A second light was added, but both were removed in 1948; the widow's walk was closed to the public in 1959.

Guests once viewed Old Faithful Geyser's eruptions from the rooftop. "A geyser seen in eruption under the searchlight is a most remarkable sight," a 1905 Northern Pacific Railway brochure exclaimed. Colorado Historical Society

Dormer windows pop out along the steep roofline. Logs cover the lower exterior, and redwood shingles originally covered the upper floors. The cedar-shingled roof was stained in 1910. While the Inn is often referred to as a giant log cabin, its skeleton is really modern frame construction of the day. The Inn's concrete foundation has a stone veneer quarried from the nearby Black Sand Basin. Huge cribbed-log piers supported the original porte-cochère, and the later porte-cochère addition and verandah that rests on steel columns inside log cribbing.

Guests enter the Inn through the massive red-painted doors and step center

Stone foundation, cedar-shingled siding and cribbed logs create the Inn's rustic architectural detail, above. Charred trees are reminders of the 1988 forest fire that nearly engulfed Old Faithful Inn, facing page. David Morris

Upright poles and beams of the interior support system are made of tree trunks and branches. Balconies and stairways wind through the log columns and gnarled knee-branch supports help create the Inn's forest setting. Split-log facing covers the ceiling.

Perched in the upper reaches of the room is a crow's nest. The trapeze-like platform looks like a treehouse, but provided a venue for musicians who climbed to the crow's nest to play pre- and post-dinner performances.

Originally, the bark was left on the timber, but it was peeled for easier maintenance while the lodge was closed during World War II. The forest setting survives as light dances through the atrium tree tops, then is lost in the dark recesses of gnarled lodgepole-pine that lines the mezzanine, stairways and balconies. The twisted logs and limbs seem a frivolous contrast to the business of creating a structure that could withstand twenty-foot drifts of snow and temperatures that could dip to sixty degrees below zero.

stage into the great-hall lobby. The room rises seventy-six-and-a-half feet, and each set of eyes gazes upward. Square and diamond windowpanes filter light into the great hall. The scene seems too much to absorb.

Lodgepole pine trunks and gnarled branches give the Inn's great hall its forest-like atmosphere, left. Architect Robert Reamer hand-picked many of the logs and branches. His detail work also included the design of the stairway, below, and the candle-like light fixtures, right. Fred Pflughoft & David Morris

The great hall lobby of Old Faithful Inn today, left, and the lobby pictured in a 1917 postcard, above, show the results of meticulous restoration. The Inn is a National Historic Landmark, one of five such designations in the park. Fred Pflughoft & David Morris and Yellowstone National Park, No. 31406.

The lava rock fireplace, placed on a fifteen-by-fifteen-foot base, anchors the great hall's asymmetrical design. Tapering to a modified forty-one-foot pyramid, it features four large hearths and four smaller ones in the corners. Hanging from the chimney's face is a huge fourteen-foot windup clock designed by Reamer.

As the Inn's needs evolved, the main lobby and great hall were reconfigured to make space for the necessities of tourism. The lounge around the fireplace was once sunken and set off by log railings, creating a sheltered seating area. In 1927, the ground-floor front wall was moved forward beneath the original porte-cochère to create space for an enlarged gift shop. The new space also "afforded more dancing room," and the sunken, railed fireplace lounge was filled and made part of the great hall. Earlier, guestrooms had been removed around the lobby to make space for an art shop, bellhops' desk, new registration desk and store.

Off the great hall is the dining room—a huge log cabin

The railroad cartoonist drew a series of fun-loving wildlife to add a touch of humor to the Inn. The designs were reproduced onto glass panels that divide the dining room and Bear Pit Lounge.
Fred Pflughoft & David Morris

with split logs covering the open, pitched roof and lower walls. Log trusses support the roof with gusset-plate and iron-rod supports. Iron hinges hold the heavy double doors. Blacksmith George Colpitts forged this ironwork and other pieces on site.

Formally attired diners ate family-style at long tables when the Inn first opened. The dining room could not accommodate all of the guests, so in June 1920, a temporary canvas-roofed addition to the south of the main dining room was constructed. Replacing it, the permanent and finely finished addition was completed for the 1922 season. Large windows that had flanked each side of the fireplace were converted to doors when the second dining room was added. The new dining

Formally attired diners ate family style at long tables when the Inn first opened. A second dining room was added behind the fireplace wall in 1922. Fred Pflughoft & David Morris

Oak writing desks with high spindle dividers and art glass center shades were brought from the Canyon Hotel after it was closed as furnishing for the mezzanine, facing page. Fred Pflughoft & David Morris

room's sophisticated atmosphere replaces the log cabin feel of the main dining room. Interior columns and beams, etched with designs and pictures of park wildlife, bring a refined touch of the outdoors inside.

In 1927, another room was attached to the side of the main dining room, creating what is now the Bear Pit cocktail lounge. The original Bear Pit Lounge opened in 1936, in part to celebrate the 1933 repeal of prohibition and the NPS's 1934 decision to allow the sale of alcoholic drinks in the parks. The room, now the snack bar tucked between the kitchen and west wing of the Old House, was lined with vertical-grain fir veneer. Reamer thought decorative sand-blasted designs would liven up the panels. In October 1934, he wrote the president of the Yellowstone Park Hotel Company: "I wouldn't mind adding a touch of humor to this room. If your Chicago cartoonist would rough out some of his funny bears they might be used to advantage."

The cartoonists created twelve panels of dancing, hard-drinking, card-playing, party bears along with their more refined bruin friends. A pair of ballroom-dancing moose and a ram waiter add to the rollicking four-legged lineup. The bears minus libations were used in a successful park advertising campaign. Today, some of the original wood panels are in the snack bar behind protective glass. In 1989, artists reproduced the panels in glass etchings that divide the main dining room from the cocktail lounge. A close inspection of the glass panels show that Reamer didn't have the last laugh. Writings on liquor bottles and some of the animals' "outfits" were slightly altered and modern coins were added to the scenes.

The original Old House had 140 rooms. Most of the guestrooms were down hallways off the east and west sides of the lobby. The first-floor rooms, with shared baths, featured rustic log decor, while the rooms on the floors above were finished with rough, unpainted pine boards. Only ten rooms had private baths. By the time the Old House was complete, Child had spent nearly $140,000 of the railway's

The towering center portion of the Inn, called the Old House, is bathed in the amber light of sunset, facing page. David Morris *The original Old House guestrooms, circa 1907, below, and today, right, have changed little over time.* Colorado Historical Society and Fred Pflughoft & David Morris

money on the building and another $25,000 on the furnishings.

Mission-style tables, davenports, rockers and settees, with rustic hickory tables and chairs, filled the lobby and mezzanine. Guestroom furnishings included brass, iron, or wood beds, natural or green finished dressers, chairs and nightstands, desks, chamber pots and wash-stands. Doubled, oak, writing-desks with high spindle dividers and art glass center shades were brought from the Can-yon Hotel after it was closed, and offer the per-fect place for visitors to make journal entries or write letters about the wonders of what is just outside the door.

The 1906 Haynes Guide to the park ex-claimed: "Old Faithful Inn, the most extensive

*Guests can relax on the mezzanine level with a
view of the lava stone fireplace and windup clock
designed by architect Robert Reamer.*
Fred Pflughoft & David Morris

log structure yet devised by man, with
every convenience and luxury of the
modern hotel, is the latest triumph in
utilizing primitive material in constructing
so unique a building. The rough blocks of
stone which form its foundation appear as
natural as when found at the base of the
cliffs of the surrounding mountains…The
interior is surprising for the grandeur of
vast forests conquered."

The Inn was an immediate success, and
soon had to be expanded. Reamer designed and supervised the construction of
the east wing addition in 1913-14, adding
one hundred guestrooms at about $1,000
each. The wing's flat tar-and-gravel roof
offered little competition to the Old House
and its spectacular pitched roof. Redwood
shingles covered the exterior walls, but the
interior offered a very different atmosphere. Plaster, not wood, covered the
walls. The furnishings were simple and
rather plain. In 1927, Reamer designed a
west wing addition with 150 rooms and 95
bathrooms at a cost of over $200,000. It
was not a pleasant experience, but what

would follow was even more troubling to
the architect.

Since the building of the Inn and first
wing, the National Park Service (NPS) had
been established, and with it a Landscape
Engineering Division that became involved
with Old Faithful Inn. Reamer's austere
second addition plans caused an immediate flap. Correspondence was exchanged
among the architect, park supervisor
Horace Albright and Harry Child, with
opinions added by other government
officials. The new wing would be more
visible than the 1913 addition, and Reamer
wanted it to be a flat-roof design so as not
to compete with the Old House. The Park
Service vehemently objected to the roof
design, and Albright wrote Child that the
addition was "…so different from the old
building that it was bound to be com-
mented on adversely." Reamer was not
impressed, and he telegraphed Child, "[I]
am just as much interested in not marring
the appearance of Old Faithful as the
government and as I designed the old
building and wasn't shot for it I according

In the spring of 1979 one of the most extensive rehabilitation projects ever made to a log structure began, which included reshingling the Old House, above. Andy Beck *Twenty years after the project began, the thousand squares of new shingles and hundreds of feet of replacement logs look like they've always been there, facing page.* Fred Pflughoft

to the code of ethics feel I should be trusted to finish the designing."

As a 200-man crew began construction, government and park officials approved the original plan, and a fourth story was added to accommodate additional bathrooms.

Over the years, repairs and alterations have kept the Inn operating. But by the late 1970s, time had taken a heavy toll on the grand log and frame structure. Rotting logs, worn shingle siding and a deteriorating roof were the obvious problems. Inside, the lobby, once a soaring stately atrium, was shabby, its space poorly adapted, and health and safety issues needed to be addressed throughout the hotel.

In the spring of 1979 one of the most extensive rehabilitation projects ever made to a log structure began. Old Faithful Inn would be brought back to its glory days under the direction of the National Park Service's Denver Service Center, in a cooperative effort with the park's new concessionaire, TW Services, Inc. That transformation took ten years and cost $7,350,000. Historians, architects, engineers, contrac-

Old Faithful Inn is closed for the winter, but snow can surprise spring guests covering the Inn in a blanket of fresh flakes. Fred Pflughoft

tors, carpenters and craftspeople pooled their talent and resolve to research, analyze and execute the undertaking.

Historic preservation guidelines were meticulously adhered to as workers began with the roof and worked their way down and through the huge wooden Inn. When a log needed to be replaced, its location, shape and cuts were determined by studying historic photos. Portions of the massive Inn were jacked up at the foundation in order to replace logs. Ornamental shingles were individually photographed, measured, drawn and hand-cut to the original design. Replacements for the gnarled branch-knee braces and lodgepole pine logs that always gave the Inn its character were searched out to replace decayed originals. Over 1,000 squares of shingles and hundreds of feet of logs were replaced.

Since the Inn was an operating hotel, most of the work was done during the off-season. Brutal weather conditions with driving blizzards and 35-degree-below-zero Fahrenheit temperatures challenged the crew, yet work was never called off due to weather. Instead, supervisors and crews devised on-site work strategies. For example, original drawings were unmanageable particularly while roofers were perched on the 45-degree pitch of the soaring roof, so mini-drawings were created on waterproof paper that slipped into workers' pockets.

Rehabilitation of the interior was not meant to bring the Inn back to one particular time period, but rather to integrate health and safety improvements and better utilize public spaces in such a way that any new additions blended with the old.

The process also provided an opportunity to repair damaged portions of the Inn. The stone fireplace on the south dining room wall, which had collapsed in 1959 during the 7.5 earthquake, was rebuilt to its original design with a new internal steel

A Yellowstone Park wolf walks through the winter landscape. John L. Hinderman

frame. This was completed in 1988, with a historical blacksmith re-creating the firescreen. The dining room fireplace and the brick portion of the chimney above the great hall were the only two notable victims of that quake or of the almost-indiscernible quakes that rumble through the park daily.

In 1988, Old Faithful Inn was nearly lost when Yellowstone National Park's most stunning fire roared toward the structure. Burning embers arrived five miles ahead of the flames. An exterior sprinkler system, installed the year before, drenched the roof of the Old House, and volunteers beat flames from the flat roofs of the wings and hosed them with water. As wind pushed the flames racing behind the building, the Inn survived.

The Old Faithful Inn Rehabilitation Project garnered three prestigious preservation awards: the Federal Design Achievement Award and the National Historic Preservation Award both in 1992, and the President's Award for Design Excellence in 1994. National Park Service architect Andy Beck, who served as the project architect of the restoration work, accepted the third award from President Bill Clinton at the White House. Beck shared these honors at the White House with NPS architects Paul Newman and Tom Busch who were responsible for the renovation work.

Keeping the Inn a working hotel and operating "museum" is an ongoing task. In 1992, $6 million was spent on renovating eighty-three guestrooms and public areas in the east and west wings of the Inn.

A&E Architects and River Run Interiors from Billings, Montana, in conjunction with the National Park Service and TWRS, transformed the austere guest rooms into charming rooms with full, modern bathrooms while still keeping the original sense of the place. The craftsman-style maple and wicker furnishing are faithful to the era in which the wings were built.

During renovation, the east wing was taken down to its skeleton on the inside, updated and returned to be an improved version of its original self. Some fixtures and hardware were reused, and the trimwork in the hallways, the texturing of sheet rock and the colors were all selected based on historical records. Soft yellow, cream, rust and light green never overpower the decor. Since then, a historic preservation crew of five to six people with special craft skills, trained on site with the Park Service, takes on restoration projects.

P.T. Barnum's big tops were portable affairs. But for nature's Greatest Show on Earth, the preservation of Old Faithful Inn seems an important attempt at making permanent that log and shingle reminder of our past.

Visitors take balcony seats on the Inn's verandah where they watch the enduring encore performance of Old Faithful Geyser. Fred Pflughoft

"This is one of the most accommodating geysers in the basin, and during our stay played once an hour quite regularly. On account of its apparent regularity, and its position overlooking the valley, it was called by Messrs. Langford and Doane "Old Faithful."-August 4, 1871, Ferdinand Hayden, *previous pages.* Fred Pflughoft *Grand architecture is not always historic. In 1999, Old Faithful Snow Lodge, below, was completed in a rustic design not meant to compete with its neighbor, Old Faithful Inn. The Snow Lodge's interior, facing page, reflects the heritage of national park design.* AmFac Parks and Resorts

Grand architecture is not always old. In 1999, the second phase of the multi-million-dollar Old Faithful Snow Lodge was completed, replacing the old Snow Lodge behind the Inn. Designed by A&E Architects, the new facility holds true to the tenets of rustic design. The prime consideration in designing the lodge was not to upstage Old Faithful Inn, rather to complement it.

Salvaged timber was used for the framework, and like Old Faithful Inn, the Snow Lodge is basic frame structure. The 100-room lodge pays homage to Robert Reamer's eye for detail. The light fixtures are custom made and each seems to tell a story. The dining room chandeliers start from the earth and sea then reflect the moon and stars. If Reamer thought the railway cartoonist might have fun with the dancing bear motif in Old Faithful's lounge, the same can be said for those who designed the Snow Lodge's Geyser Grill. Two canoes with animals holding lanterns became part of the decorative light fixtures.

Old Faithful Snow Lodge captures the character of the Inn and the historic district. Old Faithful Historic District buildings include Old Faithful Inn, the Lower Hamilton Store, built in 1897 as a photo studio for F. Jay Haynes, and Old Faithful Lodge, built in 1918 and added onto from 1923 through 1927 under the direction of

National Park Service planner and designer, Daniel Hull and architect Gilbert Stanley Underwood. In addition to the Recreation Hall of Old Faithful Lodge, Underwood's Yellowstone work includes the 1925 dining hall in West Yellowstone. He is best known for his lodges in Bryce, Zion and Grand Canyon national parks and The Ahwahnee hotel in Yosemite National Park.

During the decade that Robert Reamer worked for Harry Child, he created numerous buildings within Yellowstone or nearby in Montana. In 1902, he designed both Old Faithful Inn and the log depot in Gardiner, Montana. His other achievements included the second Canyon Hotel, built in 1911 (slated for demolition in 1959, but mysteriously burned in 1960),

The original Lake Hotel was built in 1891, making it the oldest extant hostelry in the park. Additions and renovations have kept it an elegant reminder of the past. Fred Pflughoft

and extensive changes to the Lake Hotel. He also submitted plans for Mammoth Springs Hotel in 1909 (some were used and others never executed) and the cottages behind that hotel. In 1925, he designed four residences at Gardiner for the Yellowstone Transportation Co., plus a number of small buildings

The elegant Lake Hotel is a far cry from the simple clapboard hotel that opened in 1891. Child hired Reamer in 1904 to transform the standard railway building into a neoclassical hotel. By extending the roofline, adding imposing ionic columns, introducing faux balconies and altering the window, Reamer transposed the hotel from dull to delightful. In the 1920s, an annex and new dining room were added and Reamer remodeled the lobby. The focal point of his work was the design of the fireplace using Arts and Craft motifs on the hearth. In 1928,

Beginning in 1904, Old Faithful Inn's architect Robert Reamer gave the ordinary Lake Hotel neoclassical charm by extending the roofline and creating a sense of arrival using columns, gables and decorative moldings. Colorado Historical Society

Reamer enlarged the lobby and added a porte-cochère. Interior renovation was done in 1987.

These are just a few of the over 1,000 historic structures within the park including Fort Yellowstone in the Mammoth Hot Springs Historic District, the first buildings constructed to house the Army in 1891.

A Visitor Education Center in historic national "parkitecture" design is planned for the Old Faithful area, proving that buildings that look old can be very new.

Yellowstone National Park

While Old Faithful Inn and the structures of the park are man-made reminders of our past, ninety-nine percent of the park's 2.2 million acres is undeveloped. Yellowstone's 10,000 thermal features total more geo-thermal activity than in the rest of the world combined. The twenty-five named geysers in the Upper Geyser Basin, home of Old Faithful Geyser, comprise the largest concentration of geysers on the globe.

Bear, big horn sheep, bison, bobcats, porcupines, beavers, coyotes, moose, elk, deer and, of course, gray wolves are some of the fifty mammals that roam the vast region and are as famous as the spewing geysers and bubbling mud pots. There are 309 recorded species of birds, eighteen types of fish and six varieties of reptiles.

Two hundred and thirty waterfalls careen from faces of rock including the highest, the Lower Falls of the Yellowstone River with its 308-foot drop. Yellowstone Lake is one of the coldest, largest and highest lakes in North America. Mountains reach over 11,000 feet with meadows and range spilling across the landscape.

Eighty percent of the park is forest with eight species of conifers, predominately

lodgepole pine. Wildflowers bloom from April into September.

Annually, over three million visitors wind their way over the park's 466 miles of roads or hike on the 1,000 miles of backcountry trails. With each curve in the road or trail, each sighting of a bison or bear, each geo-thermal wonder, they experience what Ferdinand Hayden felt in 1871 when he wrote, "…the beholder stands amazed…at nature's handiwork."

The sun rises over the Yellowstone River near Alum Creek, facing page, and the Grand Prismatic Spring at Midway Geyser Basin, right, are all part of the wonders of Yellowstone National Park.
Fred Pflughoft

The author wishes to thank the architects, historians and archivists with the National Park Service, particularly Andy Beck, Susan Kraft, Paul Newman and Lee Whittlesey and Jim Bos (A&E Architects), Barry Cantor (TWRS) and Tamela Whittlesey.

The strange beauty of Great Fountain Geyser, previous pages, Fred Pflughoft, *and the playfulness of a young grizzly as he paws a dead sapling, left,* John L. Hinderman, *illustrate the incredible diversity within the park.*

Albright, Horace and Robert Cahn. *The Birth of the National Park Service: The Founding Years, 1913-33* (Salt Lake City, 1985).

Bartlett, Richard. *Yellowstone: A Wilderness Besieged* (Tucson, 1985).

___. *Great Surveys of the American West* (London and Norman, 1962).

___. 1970 correspondence from Jane Reamer White to Richard Bartlett, courtesy of Richard Bartlett.

Dittl, Barbara and Joanne Mallmann. *The Story of the Lake Hotel* (Boulder, 1987).

Haines, Aubrey L. *The Yellowstone Story: A History of Our First National Park.* 2 Vols. (Boulder, 1977).

Harrison, Laura Soulliere. *Architecture in the Parks, National Historic Landmark Theme Study* (National Park Service, Washington, D.C., Nov. 1986).

Hyde, Anne Farrar. *An American Vision: Far Western Landscape and National Culture, 1820-1920* (New York and London, 1990).

Hubbard, Freeman. *Encyclopedia of North American Railroading: 150 Years of Railroading in the United States and Canada* (New York, 1981).

Kaiser, Harvey H. *Landmarks in the Landscape* (San Francisco, 1997).

Shea, Paul Gilbert Stanley Underwood: *His Cafeterias and the Montana Connection,* (Paper presentation, Nov. 1999).

Tweed, William; Laura E. Soulliere; Henry G. Law. *National Park Service Rustic Architecture: 1916-1942* (National Park Service, Western Regional Office, Feb. 1977).

Yellowstone National Park Archives, Mammoth, WY. Box C-14, file 332.2, YPHCo., 1925-27; YPC-14, lodges and camps, 1932-37; YPC-34, business correspondence, 1934-36; YPC-126, Old Faithful Inn, 1959; Letter box #39, file #10, accommodations at hotels and camps; Superintendent (or Acting) Annual Reports 1890, 1899, 1901 and 1904; *Through Wonderland*, Northern Pacific Railway brochure, 1905; YPC, Volume 3 (furniture) Inventory, Sept. 30, 1929, The American Appraisal Co.; Clemensen, A. Berle. *Historic Structure Report, Old Faithful Inn, Yellowstone National Park* (NPS, Denver) 1982; historical photos.

Montana Historical Society Photo Archives, Helena, MT, and Colorado Historical Society Photo Archives, Denver, CO.

National Park Service, Denver Service Center, CO: *Old Faithful Inn Rehabilitation Project, Yellowstone National Park, Wyoming, Presidential Design Awards 2000 Nomination form*; Beck, Andy, *National Park Service Stories, The Greatest Log Cabin Restoration, The Old Faithful Inn, Yellowstone National Park, Wyoming, 1993; National Historic Preservation Awards—1991*.

Hotel Reservations:

Old Faithful Inn and all in-park lodging reservations are available through Amfac Parks and Resorts (307) 344-7311. Old Faithful is open from May to mid-October.

Directions:

Old Faithful Inn is located in the southwest portion of Yellowstone National Park in Wyoming. The Old Faithful Area is southeast of Madison from the West Yellowstone, MT entrance or northwest of West Thumb from the south entrance in Wyoming. The park's two seasons run from mid-April to late-October and mid-December to mid-March. Commercial airline service is from Cody and Jackson, WY and Bozeman, MT. The West Yellowstone, MT airport is open from June to early September. Public transportation is not available in the park, and most visitors travel by personal vehicles. Bus tours in the summer and snow-coach tours are available in the winter.

The park's official website is www.nps.gov/yell/

A pelican floats on Yellowstone River near Fishing Bridge. Fred Pflughoft